Introduction, Theme and Variations

for Flute and Piano

Louis Moyse

ED 3351
March 2000 Printing

ISBN 0-634-01556-7

G. SCHIRMER, Inc.

DISTRIBUTED BY

HAL•LEONARD®
CORPORATION
7777 W. BLUEMOUND RD. P.O. BOX 13819 MILWAUKEE, WI 53213

To André Jaunet

INTRODUCTION, THEME AND VARIATIONS

Introduction

Louis Moyse

48377c

48377

*Thumb on B – trill A B (third finger) **Little key trill – (fourth finger) φ both flutter and trill

legato – tenuto by fingers (with pedal)

*E: Little finger off (sounding like harmonic)

THEME

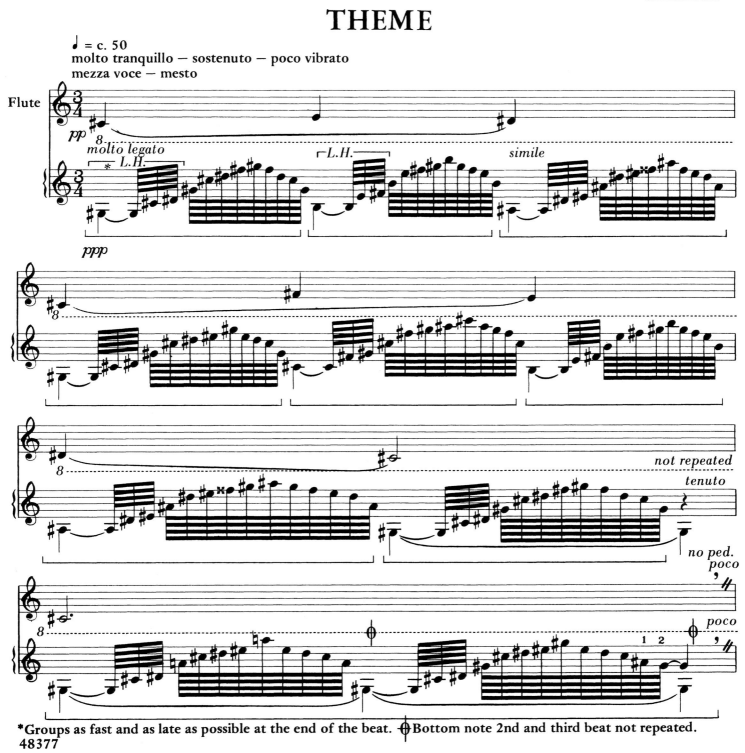

*Groups as fast and as late as possible at the end of the beat. ⊕Bottom note 2nd and third beat not repeated.

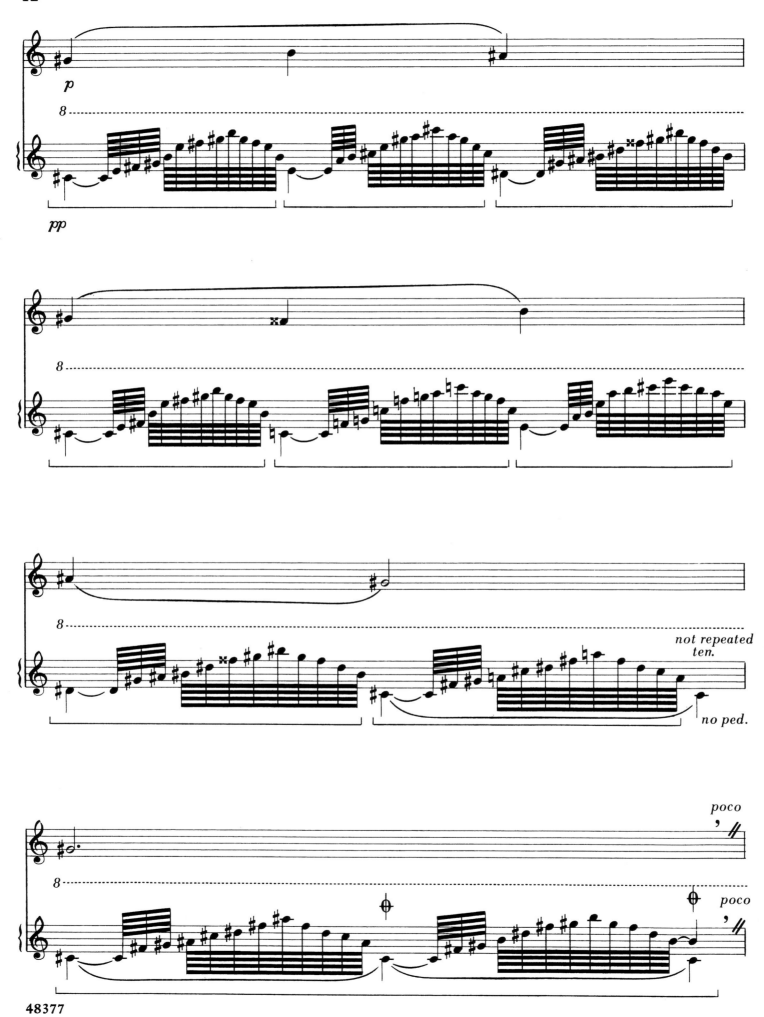

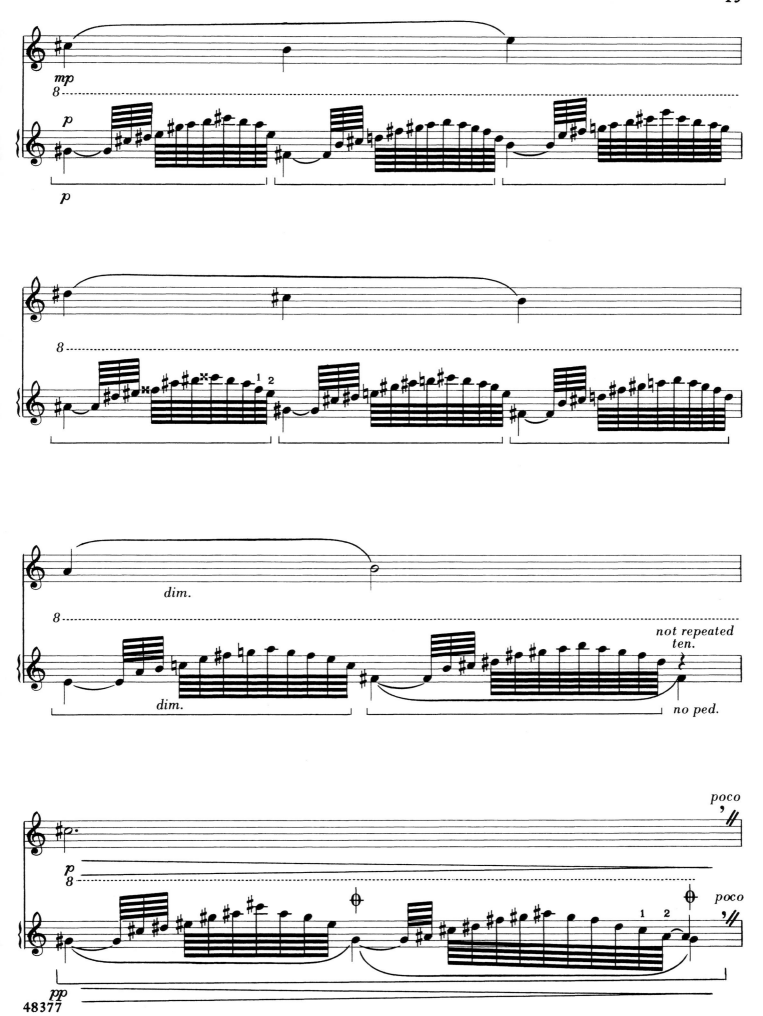

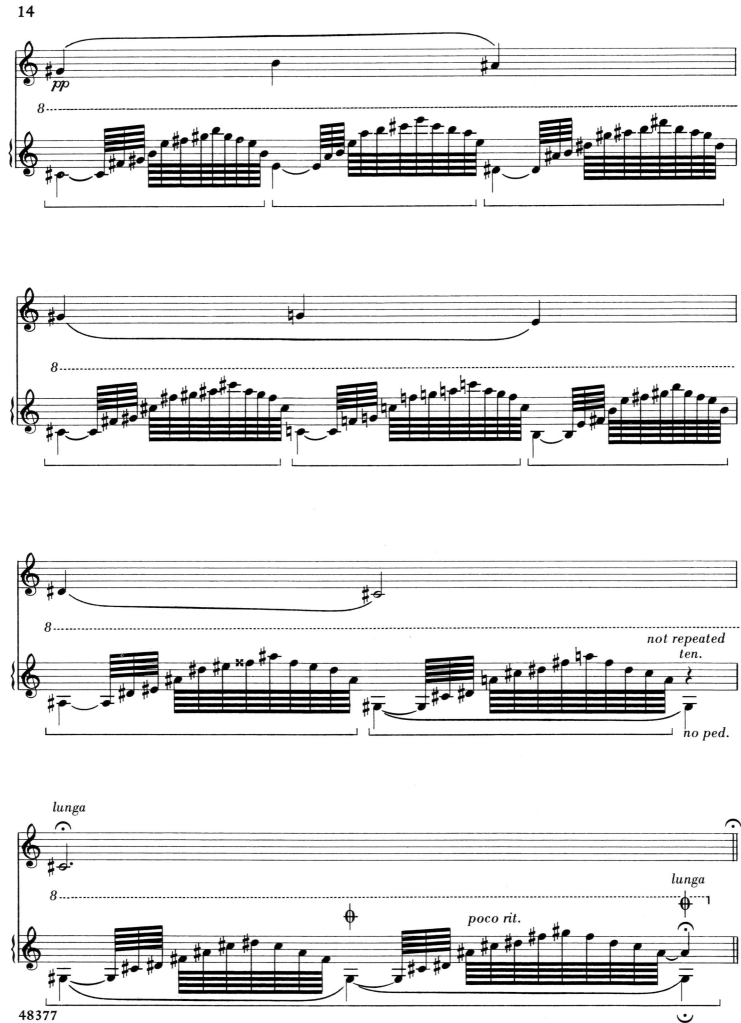

VARIATION I

*Sixteenths, light and rather shorter than their values.

Introduction, Theme and Variations

for Flute and Piano

Louis Moyse

Flute

ED 3351
March 2000 Printing

ISBN 0-634-01556-7

G. SCHIRMER, Inc.

DISTRIBUTED BY

HAL•LEONARD®
CORPORATION

7777 W. BLUEMOUND RD. P.O. BOX 13819 MILWAUKEE, WI 53213

INTRODUCTION, THEME AND VARIATIONS

Introduction

Flute

Louis Moyse

*Thumb on B — trill A B (third finger)   **Little key trill — (fourth finger)   φ both flutter and trill

* E: Little finger off (sounding like harmonic)

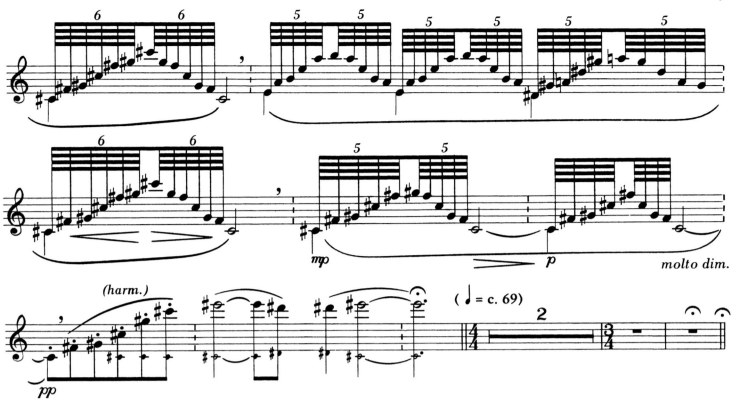

THEME

8

VARIATION I

VARIATION II

*Sixteenths, light and rather shorter than their value.

VARIATION III

VARIATION IV

VARIATION V

VARIATION VI

*Groups of triplets *rapido*

VARIATION VII

VARIATION III

*Sixteenths, left hand strictly in time rhytmically.

21

48377

VARIATION IV

48377

VARIATION V

48377

VARIATION VI

*Groups of triplets *rapido*.

VARIATION VII

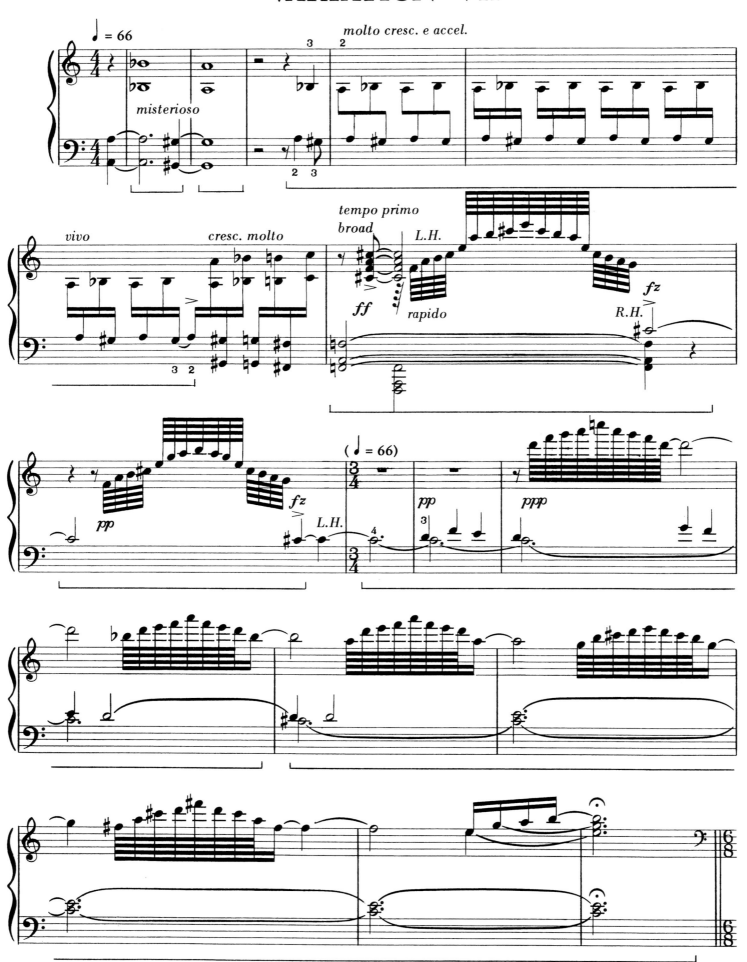

48377